Dinosaur Detectives
Search for the facts...

Placodus
and Other
Swimming Reptiles

Tracey Kelly

raintree

a Capstone company — publishers for children

Raintree is an imprint of Capstone Global Library Limited, a company incorporated in
England and Wales having its registered office at 264 Banbury Road, Oxford, OX2 7DY –
Registered company number: 6695582

www.raintree.co.uk
myorders@raintree.co.uk

Text: Tracey Kelly
Designer: John Woolford
Design Manager: Keith Davis
Editorial Director: Lindsey Lowe
Children's Publisher: Anne O'Daly
Picture Manager: Sophie Mortimer
Production by Katie LaVigne
Printed and bound in India

ISBN 978 1 4747 7834 3 (hardback)
ISBN 978 1 4747 7840 4 (paperback)

British Library Cataloguing in Publication Data
A full catalogue record for this book is available from the British Library.

Acknowledgements
We would like to thank the following for permission to reproduce photographs:
Public Domain: G. hedoghedo/Staatliches Museum Stuttgart 4.

Every effort has been made to contact copyright holders of material reproduced in this book. Any omissions
will be rectified in subsequent printings if notice is given to the publisher.

All the internet addresses (URLs) given in this book were valid at the time of going to press. However, due to the
dynamic nature of the internet, some addresses may have changed, or sites may have changed or ceased to
exist since publication. While the author and publisher regret any inconvenience this may cause readers, no
responsibility for any such changes can be accepted by either the author or the publisher.

Contents

How do we know about dinosaurs?

Scientists are like detectives.

They look at fossils.

Fossils tell us where dinosaurs
and other ancient animals lived.

They tell us how big they were.

This skeleton is *Placodus*.
It is a swimming reptile.
It is 240 million years old.
You might see one in
a museum!

How to use this book

This tells you what the animal ate.

🌿 Plant eater

🦖 Meat eater

This tells you when the animal lived.

240 million years ago

SWIMMING REPTILES

🦖 **Placodus**

Say it! (PLAK-oh-duss)

Placodus was not a good swimmer!
It had a chunky body and a short head.
Placodus walked slowly on the shore.
It grabbed shellfish off rocks.

🌿 **MINI FACTS**
Placodus had strong teeth. They could crunch shellfish.

strong legs

swishing tail for balance

heavy body

clawed feet

FACT FILE

NAME: *Placodus* means 'flat tooth'
WEIGHT: about 200 kilograms (440 lb)
FOOD: shellfish
HABITAT: shallow waters near coasts

How big am I?

2 m (6 ft)

First found in ...
France, 1833

18   19

This shows you how big the animal was.

A map shows where the first fossils were found.

Read on to become a dinosaur detective!

5

Swimming reptiles

Large reptiles swam in the ocean.
Smaller reptiles swam in ponds and rivers.
They lived from 300 million years ago to 66 million
years ago. Some had paddles to help them swim.
Some had strong legs. They could crawl
across land. They hunted fish
and animals.

Champsosaurus

(Say it!) (KAMP-so-SAW-rus)

Champsosaurus looked like a crocodile.
It had a long jaw full of teeth. It lay
at the bottom of ponds and grabbed fish.

strong jaws with
sharp teeth

strong neck

legs stuck out
to the sides

MINI FACTS

The females laid their eggs on land. Males stayed in the water.

FACT FILE

NAME: *Champsosaurus* means 'crocodile reptile'

WEIGHT: 27 kg (60 lbs.)

FOOD: fish

HABITAT: rivers and swamps

strong tail with narrow tip

How big am I?

1.5 m (5 ft.)

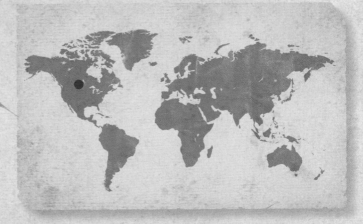

First found in ...
North America, 1876

Ichthyosaur

Say it! (ICK-thee-oh-SORE)

Ichthyosaurs were sea reptiles.
They looked like dolphins.
Some were big. Some were small.
They ate fish and sea creatures.

strong
tail for
swimming

MINI FACTS

Ichthyosaurs did not lay
eggs. They gave birth to
live babies!

How big am I?

0.3–21 m (1–69 ft.)

fin helped
steering

FACT FILE

NAME: Ichthyosaur means 'fish lizard'
WEIGHT: up to 27 tonnes (30 tons)
FOOD: fish, squid and small sea creatures
HABITAT: the ocean

pointed snout

flippers

First found in ...
England, 1811

Kronosaurus

 Say it! (CROW-no-SAW-rus)

Kronosaurus was a large reptile. It had a big head. It had four paddles. *Kronosaurus* ate fish and squid. It ate turtles too.

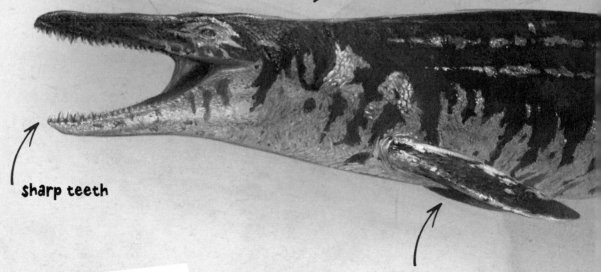

large head

sharp teeth

powerful front flippers

MINI FACTS

Kronosaurus could eat almost anything. Its teeth were as big as bananas!

 How big am I?

10 m (33 ft.)

FACT FILE

NAME: *Kronosaurus* means 'Kronos lizard'

WEIGHT: 9 tonnes (10 tons)

FOOD: large fish, squid, turtles and other swimming reptiles

HABITAT: the ocean

tail helped
steer animal

paddles for
swimming

First found in ...
Australia, 1899

13

Liopleurodon

Say it! (LIE-oh-PLOO-ro-don)

Liopleurodon was large. It had a long snout. It had sharp teeth. This reptile swam very fast! It chased large sea animals.

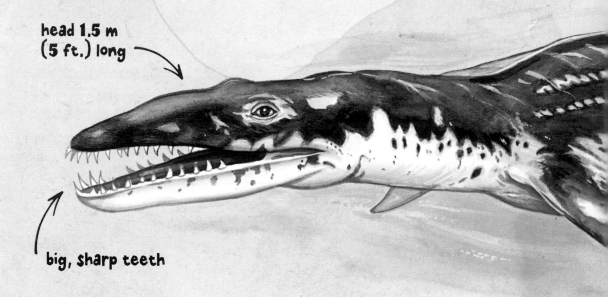

head 1.5 m (5 ft.) long

big, sharp teeth

How big am I?

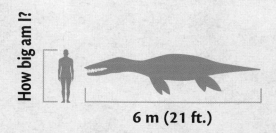

6 m (21 ft.)

FACT FILE

NAME: *Liopleurodon* means 'smooth-sided tooth'

WEIGHT: 1.7 tonnes (1.8 tons)

FOOD: fish and other sea animals

HABITAT: the ocean

long body and short tail

 **MINI FACTS**

Liopleurodon ate lots of food. It mostly ate fish.

flippers for fast swimming

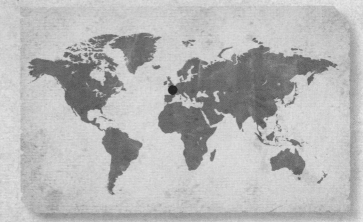

First found in ... France, 1873

15

Peloneustes

 (PEL-oh-NEW-steez)

Peloneustes was the size of a dolphin.

It had a large head and a short neck.

Peloneustes was a fast swimmer.

It hunted squid and small prey to eat.

MINI FACTS

Peloneustes had a narrow mouth. It could only eat small creatures.

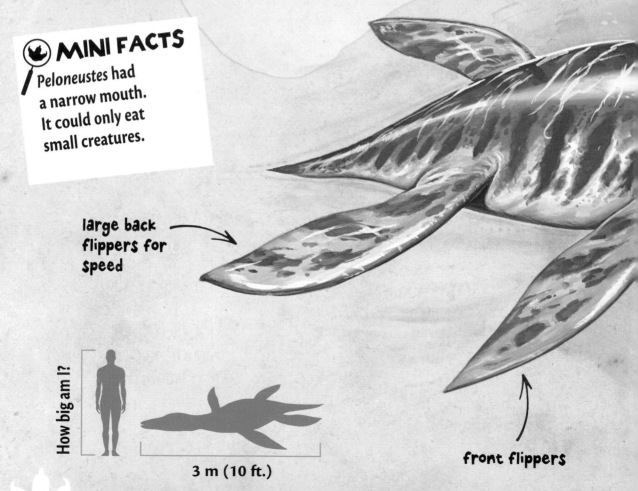

large back flippers for speed

front flippers

How big am I?

3 m (10 ft.)

FACT FILE

NAME: *Peloneustes* means 'mud swimmer'
WEIGHT: 300 kg (660 lbs.)
FOOD: fish, squid and shellfish
HABITAT: shallow seas

long snout and
sharp teeth

short neck

First found in ...
England, 1869

17

Placodus

(Say it!) (PLAK-oh-duss)

Placodus was not a good swimmer!
It had a chunky body and a short head.
Placodus walked slowly on the shore.
It grabbed shellfish off rocks.

MINI FACTS

Placodus had strong teeth. They could crunch shellfish.

strong legs

clawed feet

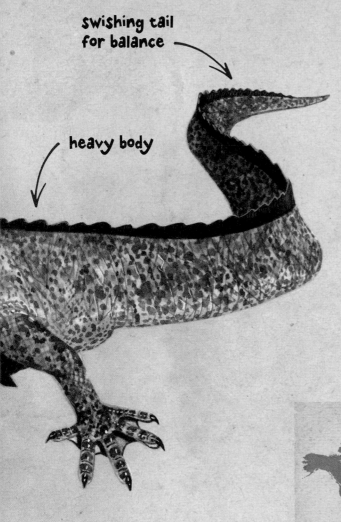

swishing tail for balance

heavy body

FACT FILE

NAME: *Placodus* means 'flat tooth'

WEIGHT: about 200 kg (440 lbs.)

FOOD: shellfish

HABITAT: shallow waters near coasts

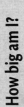

How big am I?

2 m (6 ft.)

First found in ...
France, 1833

19

Plesiosaurus

(Say it!) (PLES-ee-oh-SORE-us)

Plesiosaurus lived in the sea.
But it came up to breathe air!
It chased prey and grabbed it
with curved teeth.

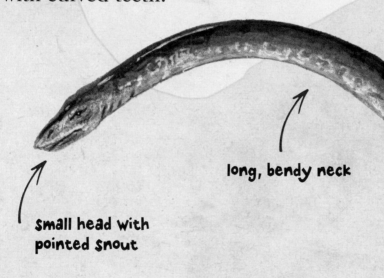

long, bendy neck

small head with
pointed snout

How big am I?

3 m (10 ft.)

paddles for
swimming

 **MINI FACTS**

Plesiosaurus came onto beaches to lay its eggs. Sea turtles do this today.

FACT FILE

NAME: *Plesiosaurus* means 'nearly a lizard'

WEIGHT: 450 kg (0.5 tons)

FOOD: fish, squid and small animals

HABITAT: shallow oceans and seas; laid eggs on sandy beaches

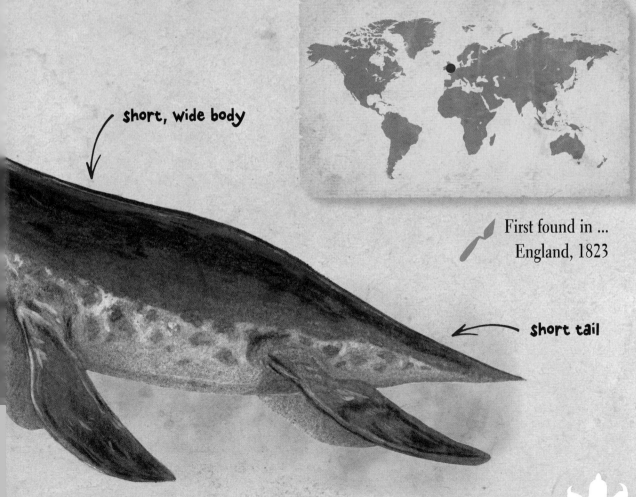

short, wide body

First found in ...
England, 1823

short tail

21

Dinosaur quiz

Test your dinosaur detective skills!
Can you answer these questions?
Look in the book for clues.
The answers are on page 24.

2 Which reptile was the size of a dolphin?

1 Which reptile grabbed shellfish off rocks?

3 Which reptile looked like a crocodile?

4 Which animal had a long, bendy neck?

Glossary

fossil
Part of an animal or plant in rock. The animal or plant lived in ancient times.

habitat
The kind of place where an animal usually lives.

paddles
Limbs that help a reptile swim underwater.

prey
An animal that is hunted by other animals for food.

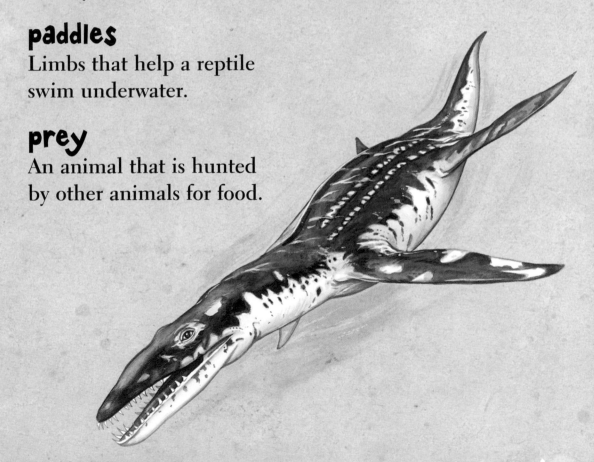

Find out more

Books

Dinosaurs (Collins Fascinating Facts),
Collins Editors (Collins, 2016)

The Usborne Big Book of Dinosaurs,
Alex Frith, (Usborne, 2017)

Websites

www.bbcearth.com/walking-with-dinosaurs/modal/plesiosaurus

www.natgeokids.com/uk/play-and-win/games/dinosaur-memory

www.nhm.ac.uk/discover/dino-directory

Index

Quiz answers: 1. *Placodus* grabbed shellfish off rocks. **2.** *Peloneustes* was the size of a dolphin.
3. *Champsosaurus* looked like a crocodile. **4.** *Plesiosaurus*.